Roberto Clemente

YOUNG BASEBALL HERO

Roberto Clemente

YOUNG BASEBALL HERO

by Louis Sabin
illustrated by Marie DeJohn

Troll Associates

Library of Congress Cataloging-in-Publication Data

Sabin, Louis.
  Roberto Clemente: young baseball hero / by Louis Sabin;
illustrated by Marie DeJohn.
     p.   cm.
  Summary: A biography of the great Puerto Rican-born baseball
player.
  ISBN 0-8167-2509-8 (lib. bdg.)   ISBN 0-8167-2510-1 (pbk.)
  1. Clemente, Roberto, 1934-1972—Juvenile literature. 2. Baseball
players—United States—Biography—Juvenile literature.
[1. Clemente, Roberto, 1934-1972. 2. Baseball players. 3. Hispanic
Americans—Biography.] I. DeJohn, Marie, ill. II. Title.
GV865.C45S23 1992
796.357′092—dc20
[B]   91-17851

Roberto Clemente

YOUNG BASEBALL HERO

The Pittsburgh Pirates were ahead by a score of 1-0 in the top of the seventh inning. But that wasn't much of a lead against a hard-hitting team like the San Francisco Giants. And now the Giants' best hitter was up at bat.

The Pirate pitcher whipped a fastball toward the plate. The batter swung and connected, sending the ball bulleting toward the right-field wall.

At the *crack!* of bat against ball, the right fielder, Roberto Clemente, whirled and raced toward the wall. Clemente's left arm reached up and the ball smacked into his glove. Then Clemente himself smacked into the concrete wall. Blood spurted from his cut chin.

Clemente fell to his knees, stunned. He shook his head to clear it. Then he raised the glove, showing the white ball nestled in the brown leather pocket. The crowd went wild. "Arriba! Arriba!" thousands of Pittsburgh fans screamed. The jubilant cry followed him every step of the way back to the Pirate dugout.

"Arriba!" was the hometown fans' way of telling Roberto Clemente just how much they loved him. By cheering him in Spanish, the fans were saying something special to the great Puerto Rican-born ballplayer.

For Roberto Clemente, the hometown fans' approval was very important. Baseball was his life, and he wanted to be a perfect player every inning of every game. He was proud when he did well. He felt very happy when his fans appreciated what he was doing for them.

Pride and hard work were a big part of Roberto Clemente. They were also the source of his family's strength. Hard work was a Clemente tradition. For as long as they could remember, the family was admired for doing a job well.

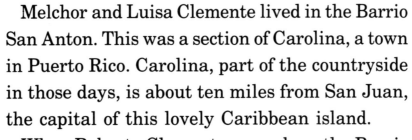

Melchor and Luisa Clemente lived in the Barrio San Anton. This was a section of Carolina, a town in Puerto Rico. Carolina, part of the countryside in those days, is about ten miles from San Juan, the capital of this lovely Caribbean island.

When Roberto Clemente was a boy, the Barrio San Anton had tiny, twisting streets dotted with small, modest houses. Everyone in the barrio was poor, but the district was not a slum. Like the rest of Carolina, its people were hard-working laborers and shopkeepers.

Sugar cane provided the main source of employment for Carolina's citizens. They labored in the fields, planting, cutting, and gathering the cane. They loaded and drove the wagons that carried the cane to processing plants. They worked in the plants, turning the crop into sugar to be shipped all over the world.

Melchor Clemente, Roberto's father, was in charge of a crew of cane-cutters. It was his job to see that the men worked well and earned their pay. He also made sure that the crew was treated fairly by the sugar company's management.

Melchor was a quiet, thoughtful, even-tempered man. The workers respected him. So did his family. "Honor comes from what you are, not what you possess," Mr. Clemente often said. His rules for living were firm: You paid back any money you owed. You had dignity, and you contributed to the well-being of your family. You also helped others less fortunate than you.

Luisa Clemente, Roberto's mother, also set high standards. She was deeply religious, warm-hearted, and devoted to her family. Together, Luisa and Melchor were wonderful parents to their children. Two of them, Luis and Rosa Maria Oquendo, were Luisa's children from her first marriage. Their father died when they were still toddlers. But Melchor Clemente treated them as his own. The Clementes also had five boys: Oswaldo, Justino, Andres, Martino, and Roberto.

Roberto, the youngest, was born at home on August 18, 1934. He was a strong, healthy, handsome baby. He was the pet of the family, but that did not spoil him. His brother, Martino, remembered Roberto's childhood clearly. "Basically, Roberto was a good kid. He did two things, played ball and stayed home. He never got into trouble. He was always quiet, never got spanked. We used to kid him about that."

The family's nickname for Roberto was Mome (pronounced Mo-may). Nobody recalled how he got the name. The word didn't mean anything, but it caught on. Soon everyone called him Mome. Roberto liked it, so he used that name when he started school.

The Clemente home was comfortable and roomy enough for the large family. There was a living room, dining room, kitchen, five bedrooms, and a shady front porch. There was even an indoor bathroom. It was unusual at that time to have indoor plumbing in the barrio.

Mr. and Mrs. Clemente worked long and hard to give their children a good home. In his job as foreman, Mr. Clemente earned three or four dollars a week. That was not much money even then, so the Clementes did other work, too.

Mr. Clemente bought an old truck. He used it to carry meat and other food, which he sold in his spare time. He drove around Carolina, stopping at houses and selling the food. His truck was like a traveling grocery store. Mr. Clemente also rented the truck to local merchants and businesses.

Mrs. Clemente earned money by doing laundry at the home of the owner of the sugar-cane factory. But she did not like to leave her children during the day. So she went to work in the middle of the night, when Mr. Clemente and the children were asleep.

It was the time of the Great Depression, and life was difficult in the barrio. Nobody had much money. Sugar cane was harvested from Christmastime until early summer. Most of the next year's crop was planted during the same months. During this time, the people of Carolina earned most of their small incomes. But from summer until Christmas there was no work. It was called *el tiempo muerto*—"the dead time."

During "the dead time," people in the barrio survived by growing vegetables in their gardens. Many families also kept chickens. The chickens supplied eggs and meat. Fishing added food to the daily diet.

Mr. Clemente did not rest during "the dead time." That was when he sold food from his truck. Often his customers had no money to pay him. He trusted them to pay their debt when they went back to work in the cane fields. And they always did.

The busy time began in November. The harvest was ready, the planting started, and the professional baseball season opened.

For little Roberto, baseball and the sugar-cane harvest marked the beginning of each year. They set the rhythm of life in the barrio. Clemente always remembered how the cane fields looked, smelled, and felt. As a boy, he liked to walk with his mother to the cane fields each day, when she brought Mr. Clemente his lunch.

To the little boy, the fields were like a green forest. The ripe sugar cane stood about fifteen feet high. The cane-cutters moved through the fields in straight lines. "Whoosh! Whoosh!" whispered their razor-sharp machetes as they chopped down row after row of stalks.

Workdays were long and tiring during the harvest season. People in the barrio woke up early, at five or six in the morning. By seven o'clock the laborers had finished their breakfasts of leftover rice and beans from the night before. They tied cords around the bottoms of their pants' legs, to prevent insects and snakes from biting them in the fields. Then they put on broad straw hats, picked up their farm tools, and gathered along the road. Soon trucks came to take them out to the fields.

Roberto Clemente never forgot the words used by his father and the other men to describe their labors. They spoke of "doing battle" with the cane, and making a living at the work was "defending yourself." It was as if the sugar-cane fields were their enemies in a never-ending war.

At 9 o'clock in the morning the workers took a break for coffee and a piece of bread. Then the cutting continued till noon, time for lunch. This meal was very important.

While the men were in the fields, the women of Carolina spent part of the morning cooking a hot meal. At noon, it was time for lunch. Each woman put the food into three or four pots or pails. One pot held stew. It was made from potatoes, yams, or corn meal, with bits of chicken or fish mixed in. Another container was filled with rice. A third one had red or white beans in a sauce. No meal was complete without rice and beans.

The workday ended by four o'clock. The men came home, where they bathed and shaved. After that it was time to relax, listen to the radio, and play baseball.

Roberto was a good child. He was quiet and respectful. There was only one thing that led him to be naughty or forgetful—baseball. Mrs. Clemente remembered that she had to keep him inside when the family was getting ready to go somewhere. "I would dress him up, nice and clean," she said, "and Roberto would come home full of dust and mud. I'd send him to the store on an errand, and he'd be gone for hours." Mrs. Clemente wasn't worried about Roberto, though. She knew where to find him—across the road, playing baseball.

"Roberto used to buy those rubber balls every chance he got," Mrs. Clemente said. "When he was small, he would lie in bed and bounce the ball off the walls. There were times he was so much in love with baseball that he did not want to stop playing to eat."

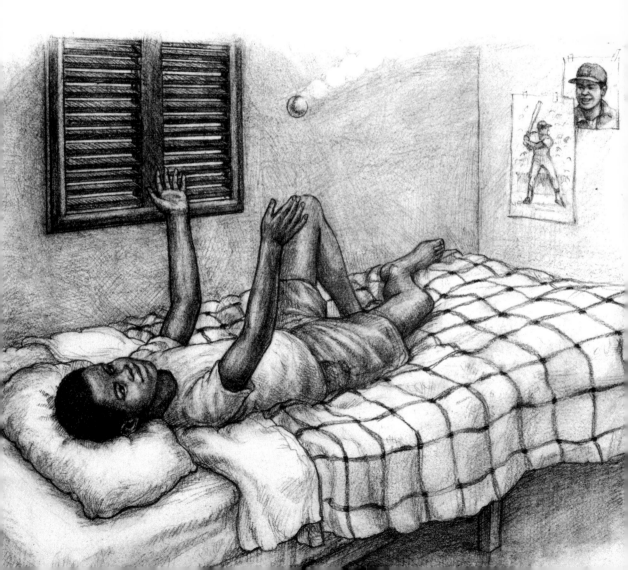

Roberto didn't only go to school and play ball. He helped his father on the truck and did household chores. He was also expected to earn his own pocket money.

When he was nine years old, Roberto asked his parents for a bicycle. "You must earn the bicycle," Mr. Clemente told him.

The boy looked hard for a way to earn money for a bicycle. The answer came when a neighbor offered him a penny a day to work for him. Roberto's job would be to carry a milk can to the country store a half mile away, fill it, and bring it back. Roberto agreed, and did the task faithfully.

"Six o'clock every morning, I went for the milk," Clemente told a reporter years later. "I wanted to do it. I wanted to have work, to be a good man. I grew up with that on my mind."

It took three years for Roberto to earn the money to pay for a used bicycle. Roberto enjoyed riding that bicycle, because he had worked so hard for it.

The climate is warm all year in Puerto Rico, and it is always comfortable to be outdoors. That is why Puerto Rican social life and games take place outdoors. People sit on their porches, playing dominoes and listening to baseball games or music. They have cookouts and outdoor dances. And the island's number-one sport is the great outdoor game, baseball.

Baseball was the best part of Roberto Clemente's childhood. "Roberto was born to be a baseball player," his mother said. Each day he ran home from the Fernandez Grammar School, drank a glass of milk and dashed outside to play.

It seemed Roberto was never without a ball in his hand. Usually, it was a rubber ball that cost only a few pennies. Whenever the ball broke or got lost, Roberto began saving his pennies for another. Meanwhile, he carried a "ball" made of crushed magazine pages wrapped in string. When he finally had enough money to buy a new ball, Roberto was happy!

Still, baseball remained *número uno* to Roberto. Night and day, he had a ball in his hand. He bounced it against walls. He threw it into the air and caught it. He squeezed it, to strengthen his hands and arms. He even kept it next to him in bed at night.

Many times the boy's love of baseball got on Mrs. Clemente's nerves. One time Roberto forgot to run an important errand for his mother. She got so annoyed that she threw his baseball bat into the wood-burning stove. Roberto cried out and snatched the bat from the flames.

When Roberto Clemente was an All-Star baseball player, he liked to tease his mother about that day. He joked that she almost ruined his career. She laughed but reminded him that he had learned a lesson. "From that day on," she said, "you never failed to do your chores."

Roberto Clemente loved his parents very much. "When I was a boy," he said, "I realized what lovely people my father and mother were. I learned from them the right way to live. I never heard any hate in my house. I never heard my father or my mother raise their voices or say a bad word to each other.

"We were poor, but we never went hungry. They always found a way to feed us. My mother fed the children first, then she and my father would eat what was left," Clemente continued. "My mother had to work hard, never went to a movie, never learned to dance. But even the way we used to live, we were happy. We would sit down and make jokes and talk and eat whatever there was. That was something wonderful."

Mr. and Mrs. Clemente wanted their children to succeed in the world. They dreamed of sending them to college. But there was no money to pay for anything more than food, clothing, and shelter. Mrs. Clemente hoped Roberto would become an engineer or an architect, because he was very good in arithmetic. He also seemed to understand what made things work and was always able to fix them.

This skill stayed with Roberto Clemente all his life. In fact, it was his hobby. Even when Clemente was a highly paid baseball player, he did all his own home repairs. "For as long as I can remember," he said, "I liked to make and fix things with my own hands."

But baseball was Roberto Clemente's greatest talent. By the time he was eight years old, he was on a real team. All the other players were two or three years older, but little Mome had no trouble making the grade. And when he wasn't playing with the neighborhood team, he played baseball with his brothers. They were all talented athletes, but Roberto was the best athlete in the family.

When Roberto was a student at the Julio C. Vizarrondo High School, he was outstanding at track and field. He competed in the javelin throw, the 400-meter dash, the triple jump, and the high jump. Roberto looked like a sure bet to make the Puerto Rican Olympic team in at least one event. But he wasn't interested in the Olympics. His devotion to baseball made everything else less important.

The athletes Roberto Clemente admired were all baseball stars. His favorite among them was Monte Irvin. Irvin, who was an outfielder for the New York Giants, played in the Puerto Rican leagues during the winter. When Roberto had twenty-five cents to spare and Irvin's team was playing in San Juan, the teenager took the bus to Sixto Escobar Stadium. The bus fare was five cents each way, and a seat in the bleachers cost fifteen cents. To sit in the sun-baked bleachers and watch his hero hit, run, and throw was Roberto's idea of a perfect day.

After the game, the boy stood outside the player's gate, waiting to see Irvin. "I never had enough nerve to look at him straight in the face," Clemente remembered. "I would wait for him to pass and then look at him. I idolized him." On August 6, 1973, Monte Irvin was inducted into baseball's Hall of Fame. On that very same day, Roberto Clemente also became a member of the Hall of Fame.

When Roberto was fourteen years old, a man named Roberto Marin spotted his outstanding ability to play baseball. Marin managed a team in the Carolina softball league. "I saw this one kid who never struck out," Marin said. "So I asked him to play for my team."

It was Roberto's first step on the road to the major leagues. He began playing for Marin's softball team, and also in the San Juan Youth Baseball League. Two years later he was starring for a San Juan team in a league that was at the level of Class A professional baseball in the United States.

By the time he was seventeen, Clemente's play caught the attention of Alex Campanis, a scout for the Brooklyn Dodgers. Roberto was one of seventy-two young hopefuls at a major-league tryout at Escobar Stadium. Campanis had all of them catch and throw from the outfield. Then he had them sprint sixty yards. After the last dash, Campanis said, "Thank you, and good-bye" to seventy-one of them.

39

The only one left was Roberto Clemente. Campanis sent a minor-league pitcher to the mound and asked Clemente to bat against him. "The kid hit line drives all over the place," Campanis said, "while I'm behind the batting cage telling myself, we've got to sign him. The kid swings with both feet off the ground and hits drives to right and sharp ground balls up the middle. How could I miss him? He was the greatest natural athlete I ever saw as a free agent!"

Roberto Clemente had everything a major-league team looks for. He had a strong arm, he ran fast, and he was a solid hitter. Equally important, he was a serious young man who was eager to learn and improve. Clemente lacked just one thing: professional experience.

On the advice of Roberto Marin, the teenager signed a contract to play winter baseball with a team called the Santurce Crabbers. They played in the Double-A Puerto Rican league. The Crabbers were stocked with seasoned pros from the U.S. major leagues and other promising rookies like Clemente. It was exactly the experience Roberto needed.

In the spring of 1954, after two fine seasons with Santurce, nineteen-year-old Roberto Clemente's career took a leap upward. He was signed by the Montreal Royals of the International League. That was only one step below the major leagues. And the next year, Clemente took the biggest step of all. He joined the Pittsburgh Pirates of the National League.

For the next eighteen years, Clemente made his mark in the record books. He won the National League batting title four times. He won twelve Gold Glove awards for fielding excellence. He was voted the National League's Most Valuable Player and the World Series MVP in 1971. He also played in twelve All-Star games.

Clemente's list of baseball records goes on and on, capped by his joining a select group of players with 3,000 or more hits in their major-league careers.

If his achievements as a player were Roberto Clemente's only claim to fame, they would be enough. But there is much more to this man's story. For Clemente was not only a great baseball player. He was also a great human being.

No matter how successful he became or how much money he made, Clemente remained the same person. He worked hard at his sport. He didn't drink liquor or smoke. He stayed up late only when Pittsburgh played a night game. Otherwise, like the sugar-cane workers of Carolina, he was in bed by ten P.M.

Roberto Clemente's whole life was baseball, his wife and children, and giving to others. He regularly visited sick children in hospitals. Friends in Puerto Rico always turned to him when they needed help, and he came through for them. Every winter, he conducted youth baseball clinics all over Puerto Rico. He took part in anti-drug campaigns and led an effort to build a large sports complex for Puerto Rican boys and girls.

On December 23, 1972, a terrible earthquake rocked the country of Nicaragua. Clemente immediately rushed to help. He went on Puerto Rican radio and television, asking for medicine, food, and clothing for the earthquake survivors. Then he chartered several planes to carry these supplies to Nicaragua.

But Roberto Clemente didn't stop at that. He wanted to make sure that the supplies reached the neediest people. So he decided to go along with the crew aboard the last plane. He left San Juan on New Year's Eve.

Then disaster struck. Clemente's plane fell into the sea, killing everyone aboard.

The shock of Clemente's sudden, tragic death was felt by people everywhere. To Puerto Ricans, it was the loss of a national hero. To his family it was the loss of a husband, a father, a son, a brother.

To baseball fans, it was the loss of a superstar. To everyone who learned of his acts of goodness, it was the loss of a fine human being.

The summer after his death, Roberto Clemente was inducted into the Baseball Hall of Fame. On this occasion, friends remembered something he had once said: "I want to be remembered as a ballplayer who gave all he had to give."

Roberto Clemente got his wish. For that is exactly how he is remembered.

DATE DUE

SEP 2 5 1992	OCT 0 6 1998	
DEC 9 1992	JA 27 03	
	JA 30 02	
	FE 13	
13	NOV 28	
NOV 1994	MAY 0 8 2006	
FEB 1995	MAY 0 8 2006	
FEB 1995	DEC 0 6 2006	
APR 25 1995		
FEB 1996		
MAY 1 5 1997		
OCT 29 1997		
APR 12 1998		
MAY 2 5 1998		
9/15/13		

Demco